Read Around the World 1

Folk Plays to Read and Record

Jane Moran

Drawings by Martin Pitts

Edward Arnold

© Jane Moran 1985

First published 1985 by
Edward Arnold (Publishers) Ltd
41 Bedford Square
London WC1B 3DQ

Edward Arnold (Australia) Ltd
80 Waverley Road
Caulfield East
Victoria 3145
Australia

British Library Cataloguing in Publication Data
Moran, Jane
　Read around the world 1: folk plays to read
　and record.
　I. Title
　428.6　PE1119

ISBN 0-7131-7395-5

Set in 11/13pt Plantin by
C.K. Typesetters, Sutton, Surrey
Printed by Spottiswoode Ballantyne, Colchester

Preface

Each of the plays in this book is based on a legend or folk-tale from a different country. There is a story from India, Scotland, Greece, Wales and the West Indies.

The vocabulary used in each play has been carefully selected with the needs of pupils within the age range of nine to twelve years especially in mind. Most pupils should be able to read the speeches without difficulty. The character parts vary in length so that more fluent pupils can take more demanding roles. Those pupils who have some degree of difficulty with reading can be allocated shorter and easier roles. The characters at the head of the cast list are more demanding parts than those at the end. This should enable the teachers to select suitable roles for their pupils' abilities. Each play has at least eight characters, some have ten or more. In this way, a large number of pupils can become involved with the readings.

After each play there are sections of follow-up work. The first section involves basic comprehension and can be answered either orally or by written work. The second section concentrates on artwork and seeks to expand the pupils' understanding of the country of origin of the story. The third section is a further test of comprehension. Section four provides a series of questions to stimulate interest in the geography of each of the countries. The final section is concerned with encouraging some research into the history or customs of each of the countries. In this section it is hoped that pupils who undertake the research will gain insight into the way in which various cultures function and develop.

The plays can be either read or recorded in the classroom. Each play lasts approximately fifteen minutes.

Contents

1 *Harisharman's Story*

Indian stories

India is a large country. It has sea on its southern, western and eastern borders. On its northern edge, it is blocked from most other European-Asian lands by huge mountain ranges. Because of its geography, India has developed customs and stories that are different from those of other countries.

India is rich in stories that go back many thousands of years. Some of these stories come from books telling tales about great and powerful heroes. Others retell the lives of the Indian gods and goddesses. Many of these stories are long and quite complicated but are beautifully written. Other stories are more simple, they come from collections of tales about animals found in India such as the mongoose, the jackel and the elephant. These stories have messages for the readers to learn how to live their lives more wisely.

Indian folk stories show quite clearly how it is possible to overcome all sorts of problems if people use their intelligence and have courage. Most of them also show that a certain amount of good fortune is also needed.

Harisharman's story

Harisharman is a poor man living in India. He is worried about his family and how they will have enough money to eat and live comfortably. He decides to get himself noticed by important people so that he can improve his position in life. At first things go very well for them all. Then Harisharman gets noticed more than he really wants.

Characters:

Narrator	**Rati,** *Rich Master's wife*
Harisharman	**Sumitra,** *Rich Master's daughter*
Rajah	**Nala,** *Rich Master's son-in-law*
Rich Master	**Jihva's Brother**
Jihva	**Rama,** *Harisharman's son*
Minister	**Indira,** *Harisharman's daughter*
Sita, *Harisharman's wife*	**Servant**

Narrator Many years ago, in the country called India there lived a man called Harisharman. He was a poor man and not very wise. This is his story.

Morning — in a small, poor house

Sita We are so poor, Harisharman, that we can no longer feed our children.

Rama And we are so hungry, father, that we can no longer walk to the town.

Indira We are so weak, father, that we can no longer keep our house clean and tidy.

Harisharman Then, my wife and dear children, I must sit and think what to do!

Narrator So he sat and thought! He decided that they must go to the Rich Master and ask him for jobs for all the family.

Later — in a large, fine house

Rich Master You, Harisharman, will be my messenger. Your wife and daughter can clean and tidy our house. Your son can look after my animals.

Harisharman Good, now everyone will be happy.

Sita You are clever, Harisharman.

Narrator Some months later there was great

8

excitement in the Rich Master's house.

Sita Have you heard the news? Our Master's daughter is to be married.

Rama There will be a big feast and so much wonderful food.

Indira There will be dancing and parties all day long.

Harisharman What an exciting time we will all have.

Narrator But no one remembered to invite Harisharman or his family to the feast or the dance.

Harisharman We have been forgotten! I feel so disappointed.

Sita It is a sad thing to be left out of all the fun and happiness.

Rama I saw all the lovely food being carried in on golden plates.

Indira And I saw all the musicians carrying their instruments.

Harisharman Then, my wife and dear children, I must sit and think what to do! (*sits down*)

Sita Have you finished thinking yet?

Rama Have you got an idea?

Indira Have you, father?

Harisharman We need to make the Rich Master notice us so we can go to the feast.

Sita How will we do that?

Harisharman You, Sita, must tell the Master's wife that I am a great magician who sees things that no one else can see.

Rama Can you, father?

Harisharman Wait and see!

Narrator At night when everyone was asleep, Harisharman crept to the stables. He took away the new son-in-law's horse and hid it. Then next day....!

Rich Master My son-in-law's horse has been stolen! What a disgrace!

9

Sumitra You must find the horse at once.

Nala It was my favourite horse.

Rati Husband, I have been told that there is a magician in our house who can see things that others cannot see.

Sumitra Then call this man to us at once.

Nala Oh yes, please do, he may get back my horse.

Rati (*shouts*) Harisharman! Harisharman, come here!

Rich Master Harisharman, come here at once!

Harisharman Do I hear my name being called?

Rich Master Yes, indeed you do. We need your help.

Harisharman I see! Yesterday when your daughter's marriage party was being held, then I was forgotten.

Rati We are very sorry, Harisharman, forgive us please.

Rich Master My son-in-law's horse has been stolen.

Harisharman Really?

Sumitra Can you truly see what others cannot see?

Harisharman Yes, of course.

Nala Can you see where my poor horse is being kept?

Harisharman It is not quite as easy as that.

Rich Master Tell me what you need and I shall send for it.

Harisharman I need to sit and think.

Narrator Then he went into the corner of the room and sat down. After a few minutes he began drawing a pattern on the floor with his fingers. Then he smiled.

Harisharman Yes! I have seen the horse.

Rich Master You are a real magician.

Rati Where is the horse?

Sumitra Is it far from here?

Nala Tell me and I shall fetch him at once!

Harisharman The animal is tied to a tree on the southern

	side of the village, near to the river.
Rich Master	Then I shall send a servant to bring the horse back.
Rati	(*shouts*) Servant, come here.
Servant	What is the Master's command?
Rich Master	Go to the south of the village and near to the river you will find my son-in-law's horse. Bring it back here.
Servant	I shall do as you ask, Master.
Narrator	The servant found the horse just where Harisharman said it would be. He brought it back to the house.
Servant	The horse has been put in the stable, Master.
Rich Master	Then you are a magician, Harisharman.
Rati	It is just as your wife said, you see things that others cannot see.
Sumitra	Thank you for making my husband happy.
Nala	You are a lucky family to have such a man in your house.
Rich Master	I shall reward you, Harisharman.
Servant	Will that be all, Master? I am tired from my long walk.
Rich Master	No, that is not all, Servant. Fetch silk and satin to make robes for Harisharman.
Servant	Then, will that be all, Master?
Rich Master	No. Then I want you to take Harisharman and his family to the great hall and give them fine food.
Servant	Then, will that be all, Master?
Rich Master	No. Then I want you to go and fetch the musicians so that they may play while Harisharman is eating.
Servant	Then, will that be all, Master?
Rich Master	Yes.
Servant	Phew!
Narrator	So everyone was happy in the Rich Master's house. Some weeks later a treasure

11

of gold and jewels was taken from the Rajah's palace. A Rajah is an Indian king. The Rajah was very upset.

Rich Master Our Rajah has asked for help to find out where his treasure is hidden.

Rati Perhaps we should tell him about Harisharman.

Narrator When the Rajah heard the story of the stolen horse, he asked for Harisharman to be sent to him.

Some days later — at the Rajah's Palace

Rajah I have heard wonderful things about you. Now I want to see your power at work.

Harisharman Oh, my Lord, I have no real power.

Rajah That is not what I have heard. I order you to find my lost treasure.

Harisharman Oh dear! I shall need time to think about it all.

Rajah You are a magician, use your power to find my treasure.

Harisharman I need to be alone.

Minister My Lord, I can take him to a room where he can be alone.

Rajah Very well, but I want an answer tomorrow, Harisharman.

Harisharman sits alone in a small room in the palace

Harisharman Oh! What a dreadful mess I'm in! I knew my tongue would get me into trouble one day. My tongue talks too much!

Narrator The Rajah had a servant girl called Jihva. The name Jihva means 'tongue'. This Jihva had helped her brother to steal the Rajah's treasure.

Outside Harisharman's small room

Jihva	Whatever shall I do? This Harisharman will know that we stole the treasure.
Jihva's Brother	Rubbish! He is no magician!
Jihva	He is! He will find out about us!
Jihva's Brother	Then we must do something about it!
Jihva	You must think of something quickly.
Jihva's Brother	Hide yourself outside this door and listen to everything that goes on.
Narrator	So, she did just what her brother had told her to do.
Harisharman	Oh, stupid tongue, foolish tongue! You're going to be punished now!
Jihva	No! Oh no! He says 'Stupid, foolish tongue, you're going to be punished!'
Harisharman	Greedy tongue, you should have been happy to stay poor and not noticed.
Jihva	There! He said it again! 'Greedy tongue!' That means me!
Narrator	So Jihva rushed into Harisharman's room and threw herself at his feet.
Jihva	(*kneeling*) I beg you, clever magician, do not tell the Rajah what you have seen.
Harisharman	What have I seen?
Jihva	That my brother and I buried the treasure by the fountain in the courtyard.
Harisharman	By the fountain in the courtyard! Well, of course, I knew the treasure was there. I've known that for some time.
Narrator	That was *not* true!
Jihva	We buried the gold and jewels but I kept some gold for myself. I will give it all to you if you promise not to tell the Rajah about us.
Harisharman	I see. Well, I shall have to think about it.
Jihva	Please!
Harisharman	I shall say nothing to the Rajah about you

Jihva and your bad brother.
Jihva Oh, thank you.
Harisharman Just fetch me the gold that you have taken yourself and I'll let you both off.
Narrator Jihva ran as fast as she could to tell her brother and get the gold.
Harisharman What luck! Here was I blaming my own tongue for my troubles when that little lady thought I was talking about her!

Early next day — Harisharman stands before the Rajah

Rajah Now you have had time to think. Tell me where my treasure is.
Harisharman I have worked hard all night. I have thought and thought and ...
Minister Tell the Rajah if the answer is that you do know where the treasure is.
Harisharman Yes.
Minister You do?
Harisharman I do.
Rajah Then tell me, where is it?
Harisharman The thief has now gone and he has taken with him some pieces of gold, but the rest of the treasure is near the fountain in the courtyard.
Rajah My servants must dig up the courtyard near the fountain. They must find my treasure.
Narrator So the servants dug in the heat of the sun and they found the treasure.
Rajah My beautiful gold and jewels! I shall reward you for this, Harisharman.
Narrator But the Minister did not trust Harisharman. He spoke to the Rajah about it, when they were alone.
Minister My Lord, you have been very good to Harisharman. You have given him gold, good food and kindness.

Rajah   Well, he did find my treasure for me.

Minister   We cannot be sure that he is an honest man though.

Rajah   What do you mean?

Minister   How do we known that he wasn't working with the thief who stole both the horse and the treasure?

Rajah   Why should he do that?

Minister   Well, my Lord, he must have known that he would be rewarded.

Rajah   Ah! I see. So you think he may not be such a clever magician after all?

Minister   We shall have to set a little test for him. One that he won't be able to wriggle out of.

Rajah   What sort of test?

Minister   I shall catch one of the frogs from near the river. I shall put it into a small jar and cover it with a cloth.

Rajah   But what has this to do with the test?

Minister   When the jar is covered, call Harisharman into the room and ask him to tell you what is in the jar.

Rajah   If he is the magician he says he is, then it will be an easy test for him.

Narrator   So Harisharman was called before the Rajah. He didn't know what to expect.

Rajah   I have a small test for you. Just so that you can show how clever you are.

Harisharman   A test, my Lord?

Rajah   I want you to tell me what is in this little jar.

Minister   The Rajah is a just man. If you tell him what is in the jar you will have a fine reward. If, however, you fail you will be horribly punished.

Narrator   Now poor Harisharman was in a dreadful mess. He had all the rewards that he wanted and the idea of a horrible punish-

	ment upset him.
Harisharman	Oh dear! Oh dear! Whatever shall I do? *(groans)*
Minister	You see, my Lord, he is not an honest man. He cannot tell you what is in the jar.
Rajah	Well, Harisharman, can you tell me?
Harisharman	I need time to think.
Rajah	You don't need time to think. My minister is right. Take him away!
Narrator	Now, there is something that you should know. When Harisharman was a child his father had given him the pet name of 'Froggy' because he was always jumping about. As he was being dragged away he called out.
Harisharman	Oh Froggy, Froggy, if your father could just see you now! Poor Froggy.
Narrator	The Rajah's eyes opened wide. The Minister stared at the jar.
Rajah	Wait! Wait! Bring Harisharman back. Did you hear what he said, Minister?
Minister	He said 'Froggy, Froggy'. I think he said that!
Rajah	He did! He knew what was in the jar all the time.
Minister	My Lord, we must be careful not to anger so great a magician.
Rajah	I know, he could use his magic against us.
Minister	Bring Harisharman back to the Rajah.
Rajah	Forgive us for testing you, Harisharman. We knew all the time how great your magic was.
Harisharman	I don't understand.
Rajah	You knew that there was a little frog, or froggy, as you called it, in the jar! How wise you are!
Narrator	Then Harisharman understood what was happening and he smiled.

Rajah I shall give you riches, gold and jewels. A State Umbrella will be held over your head whenever you go for a walk.

Minister You will be a prince, Harisharman.

Narrator So, Harisharman and his family lived in comfort. He was no longer poor. His wife and family were happy.

Some weeks later — in Harisharman's fine new home

Sita We are now so rich that we need no longer look for work.

Rama We are so well fed that I lie asleep in the sun all day.

Indira We are so happy that I dance and sing from morning until nightfall.

Harisharman And I am not stupid anymore! I shall never let anyone test my magic ever again.

Narrator And he never did.

Some questions to answer

1 Harisharman and his family were poor and they had no money to buy food. How did he try to solve the problem?

2 What exciting event took place in the Rich Master's house?

3 Why were Harisharman and his family unhappy when everyone else in the Rich Master's house was so excited?

4 Once again Harisharman tried to solve the problem. What did he decide to do this time?

5 Why did the Rajah need Harisharman's help?

6 Jihva became very upset when she heard Harisharman talking to himself. Why was she upset? What mistake had she made?

7 The Minister did not trust Harisharman, so he set a test for him to pass. How did Harisharman pass the test?

8 Why did Harisharman decide never to let anyone test his magic again?

Some things to draw or paint

1 India is a huge country, in the north there are the high mountains called the Himalayas. Other parts are covered in rain forest where tigers still live. On the coasts there are wide silver beaches with palm trees. Choose one of these different scenes and draw or paint a picture of it.

2 In India there are many beautiful temples and palaces like the one in which the Rajah lived. Draw or paint a picture of what you imagine his palace must have looked like.

3 The markets in India are always very busy and full of things to buy. They also have people there who entertain by telling stories or juggling. One sort of entertainer is the snake charmer who plays on a pipe to a snake in a basket. As he plays, the snake uncoils and moves its head in time with the pipe. Draw or paint a picture of a snake charmer and his snake.

A puzzle to solve

1 The name of Harisharman's wife.
2 This is the Rajah's servant girl.
3 This is Sita's daughter.
4 She is the daughter of the Rich Master.
5 This is Rama's father.

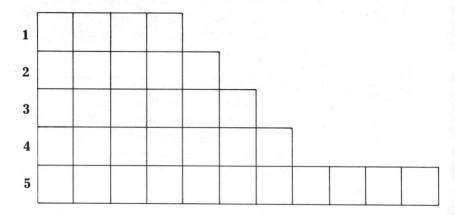

Discover : India

You will need to look at a map of India to be able to answer most of these questions.

1 When big rivers flow near to the sea they sometimes spread out over a large area. They begin to run in a number of different channels — this is called a *delta*. Look at the map of India and you will find a delta in the north east of the country at the top of the Bay of Bengal. What is the name of the river that has made this delta?

2 What is the name of the Indian city near the delta of this river?

3 Find out which is the capital city of India.

4 The highest range of mountains in the world are to the north and north east of India. What is the name of these mountains? Find out the name of the highest mountain in the range.

5 To the south east of the tip of India there is an island. Discover the name of this island and what its capital city is called.

6 Most Indian people like very hot spiced food. What is the name of the most famous of the Indian foods?

The Indian people

Although there are many different languages spoken in India, there is one official language. This is used for government documents and is spoken by nearly all of the people even though they may not use it at home. What is the name of the official language? Which is the main religion practised in India? Try to find out something about the gods and goddesses of this religion. Make a list of (a) other languages spoken in India (b) other religions practised there.

2 The White Pet

Scottish stories

Scotland is the northernmost part of Great Britain. In the past the Scots have had close links with the Scandinavian countries: Norway, Sweden and Denmark. Scottish stories have been influenced by Scandinavian folk-tales. They also have a great deal in common with Irish folk-tales, often sharing the same heroes and warriors. This is because the Scots and the Irish are part of the group of people known as the *Celts* who lived in the British Isles long before the Romans invaded the country.

Until about two hundred years ago many Scots people lived in small villages or farms well away from big towns and cities. They were mainly farmers or fishermen. In the long winter evenings, groups of people would gather together around large open fires to hear songs and tales about strange magical animals and people. Many of their stories were about heroes who lived in the isles of Scotland, or of sailors who met mermaids and great sea beasts. Other stories were centred around ordinary farmyard animals who suddenly became quite extraordinary.

The White Pet

In Scotland on a cold hillside, the little sheep called White Pet runs away to find a better life for himself. As he travels, he meets five new friends who are also running away from their homes. At the end of a long journey they have quite an adventure. The only weapon they have is their wits.

Characters:

Narrator	**Thief 1,** *the leader of the thieves*
White Pet	**Thief 2**
Bull	**Thief 3**
Dog	**Thief 4**
Cat	**Thief 5**
Chicken	**Thief 6**
Goose	

Narrator In parts of Scotland the hills are covered with purple heather and there are small stone built farms. Sheep are kept by the farmers who live here. They call their sheep 'white pets'. This is the story of how one white pet set out to find a better life for himself.

One evening in a farmyard

White Pet It is almost Christmas and I am to be killed for my master's Christmas dinner. I shall run away tonight. Baa! Baa! Baa!

Narrator When the farmer was fast asleep, White Pet slipped away from the farmyard and away over the hills.

Later — on a hillside

White Pet Safe at last! Hallo, who is that over there in the mist?

Bull I am so sad, so sad!

White Pet Why, it's the big red bull from the farm across the river. Hallo, Bull.

Bull Who's that?

White Pet It's me, White Pet. What are you doing so far from your warm shed on this cold winter's night?

Bull I have a sad tale to tell, White Pet. My master was going to kill me for his Christmas dinner.

White Pet Oh dear!

Bull So I ran away to find a better life for myself. Moo! Moo! Moo!

White Pet Poor Bull, that's just what happened to me too. Let us join together and find a better life for ourselves.

Narrator So off they went. They had only gone a little way when they saw an old black dog walking slowly towards them.

Bull Look over there, White Pet. There's Dog from the farm on the hill.

White Pet He looks very sad.

Bull His nose and tail are dragging along the ground.

White Pet What are you doing so far from your warm kennel, Dog, on this cold winter's night?

Dog I have a sad tale to tell, White Pet and Bull.

Bull Tell us your sad tale, Dog.

Dog My master said I was too old to be of use to him. I heard him say that he was going to kill me. So I ran away to find a better life. Woof! Woof! Woof!

White Pet That's just what happened to us.

Bull Join us, Dog, and together we may find a better life.

Narrator So off the three went. They had only gone a little way when they saw a thin tabby cat walking quietly towards them.

Dog Look over there. There's Cat from the poor widow's cottage.

Bull Cat looks half starved.

White Pet What are you doing so far from your warm kitchen, Cat, on this cold winter's night?

Cat Alas! I have a sad tale to tell.

Dog Tell us your sad tale, Cat.

Cat My mistress had no food left in the cottage. I heard her say she was going to drown me so I would not starve. So I ran away to find a better life. Miaow! Miaow! Miaow!

Bull That's just what happened to all of us.

White Pet	Come along with us, Cat.
Dog	Together we may find a better life.
Narrator	So off the four went. They had only gone a little way when they saw a bobbing chicken hopping along the path towards them.
Cat	Look over there. There's Chicken from the farm near the village.
Dog	Chicken looks quite cross.
Bull	Chicken is hopping towards us very fast.
White Pet	What are you doing so far from your warm coop, Chicken, on this cold winter's night?
Chicken	I have a sad tale to tell.
Cat	Tell us your sad tale, Chicken.
Chicken	My eggs have all been taken away from me. I heard the farmer's wife say that I would make a good Christmas dinner for them. So I ran away to find a better life. Cluck! Cluck! Cluck!
White Pet	That's just what happened to us.
Cat	Join us, Chicken, and together we may find a better life.
Narrator	So off the five went. They had only gone a little way when they saw a very miserable figure coming towards them.
Chicken	Look, there's Goose from the big farm near the forest.
Cat	Goose looks quite sad.
Dog	Goose is waddling very slowly.
Bull	Goose looks very lonely.
White Pet	What are you doing so far from your warm pen, Goose, on this cold winter's night?
Goose	Oh, I have a sad tale to tell.
Chicken	Then tell us your sad tale, Goose.
Goose	My poor sister was killed at Easter for the master's Easter lunch. My dear brother was killed for the mistress' birthday dinner. As Christmas is coming I know I'm next! So I ran away to find a better life. Hiss! Hiss! Hiss!
White Pet	That's just what happened to us.

Chicken Join us, Goose, and together we may find a better life.

Narrator Now there were six of them. Off they went to find the better life. The night was cold, the night was dark, the night was quiet. So they all walked in one long line with White Pet in the lead and Goose at the back. Suddenly!

White Pet Stop everyone!

Bull Why, what's wrong?

Dog What have you seen?

Cat Who have you seen?

Chicken Is it something bad?

Goose Is it something frightening?

White Pet I don't know yet. But I can see a window with a light and there is a small stone cottage.

Bull Perhaps this is where we will find our better life.

Dog We need to look into the window and see what's going on.

Cat This is exciting.

Chicken There might be danger.

Goose Well, we ought to find out.

Chicken Bull, I'll fly up and sit on your shoulder, I can see in through the window then.

Narrator So that is just what Chicken did. Bull stretched to be as tall as possible and Chicken was just able to peep inside.

Chicken Oh my! Oh my!

Bull What? What is it?

Chicken Oh my goodness!

White Pet Tell us what you've seen.

Dog What's there?

Cat What made you say 'oh my! oh my!'?

Goose Tell us, Chicken.

Chicken Shush all of you! Not so much noise! There are six, great, big, ugly thieves.

Bull Thieves?

Chicken Yes, thieves.

Dog What are they doing?

Chicken They're standing round a table and counting out a heap of gold coins.

Cat Is it a big heap of gold coins?

Chicken Yes. A very large heap of shiny gold coins.

Goose Are the thieves very big and very ugly?

Chicken Yes.

White Pet My friends, this is surely the better life that we were all looking for.

Bull Why do you say that, White Pet?

White Pet Well, they are thieves. They have got other people's money and they are wicked men. We must take the money and cottage away from such bad men.

Dog We are only six animals, we have no weapons.

Cat We aren't strong enough to drive them away.

Chicken I don't see how we can do it, White Pet.

Goose Have you a plan?

White Pet Yes, I have a plan. All of us altogether must make a great big noise. I will Baa! Bull will bellow loudly. Dog will bark. Cat will miaow. Chicken will cluck and Goose will hiss. So if you all agree, I will count us in. Ready: One, two, three...

White Pet Baa! Baa!

Bull Moo! Moo!

Dog Woof! Woof!

Cat Miaow! Miaow!

Chicken Cluck! Cluck!

Goose Hiss! Hiss!

Inside the cottage

Thief 1 What was that? (*jumps up with fright*)

Thief 2 Help us! Help us!

Thief 3 It's the devil himself!

Thief 4 Run for your life! (*runs out*)

Thief 5 Let's save ourselves before it's too late. (*runs out*)

Thief 6 Make for the woods! Make for the woods! (*runs out*)

Narrator	The six thieves ran out of the house. They ran up the hill and into the woods! The six friends cheered and went into the house.
White Pet	See, my friends, this is the better life.
Bull	Shall we divide up the gold between us?
White Pet	Yes, let's do that.
Narrator	After all the walking and the noise and the excitement, the six friends felt very tired so they decided to sleep.
White Pet	My friends, let's blow out the candles now. I shall sleep in the middle of the room.
Bull	I shall stand here behind the door.
Dog	I shall curl up in front of the fire.
Cat	I shall sleep on the table near the candles.
Chicken	I shall perch up in the rafters.
Goose	I shall settle near the door.
White Pet	Goodnight!
Bull	Goodnight!
Dog	Goodnight!
Cat	Goodnight!
Chicken	Goodnight!
Goose	Goodnight!
Narrator	Out in the cold wood, the six thieves sat and shivered. They could see the stone cottage and they saw the lights go out.

In the cold wood

Thief 2	Look, the cottage is all dark now.
Thief 3	Listen, everything is quiet now.
Thief 4	We were fools to be driven away by a noise!
Thief 5	Let's see what's going on in the cottage.
Thief 6	We'll all creep down there together
Thief 1	No! I'm the leader. I'll go and find out what's happening.
Narrator	So Thief Number 1, the leader, went slowly and carefully down the hill. He went to the cottage and he climbed in through the open window. He

felt his way to the table and reached out for the candlestick.

In the dark cottage

Cat Hallo, what's that? Take that! Take a taste of my claws! (*scratches*) Miaow!

Thief 1 Oww! Oww! My hand has been stabbed! But I must find out what's happening. I'll light the candle in the ashes of the fire. (*pokes candle into fireplace*)

Dog Hallo, what's that? Who is pushing a stick into my head? Take that! (*snaps at candle*) Howl!

Thief 1 Oh, a devil has blown out my candle! I'm getting out of here, the house is full of demons! Quick, I must run out of here! (*starts to run for the door*)

White Pet Take that! (*kicks*) My little hooves may be small but I can still kick.

Bull Take that! (*butts*) My horns and head will butt you.

Chicken Take that! (*scratches*) My claws will scratch you! Cluck! Cluck!

Goose Take that! And that! My wings will beat you hard. Hiss! Hiss!

Thief 1 Oh! Oh! To the woods, run! (*runs out of cottage*)

Narrator And that's just what Thief Number 1 did. He ran up the hill and into the woods howling and yelling dreadfully. The other thieves were waiting to hear the news.

Back in the cold wood

Thief 2 Here he comes!

Thief 3 Has he got the gold with him?

Thief 4 Look, he's running as fast as his legs will carry him!

Thief 5 Listen, he's yelling his head off!

Thief 6 Leader Thief, what's happened?

28

Thief 1 I thought my last hour had come. I got in through the window and reached out for the candle.

Thief 2 And then?

Thief 1 A man with green eyes stabbed my hand twice.

Thief 3 What happened then?

Thief 1 I managed to grab the candlestick and was going to light it in the ashes.

Thief 4 And then?

Thief 1 A rogue with huge teeth blew the candle out.

Thief 5 Then what happened?

Thief 1 There was a great bully in a thick woollen coat lying in wait and he kicked me in the shins.

Thief 6 What took place then?

Thief 1 A big fat brute behind the door took me by the seat of my pants and threw me out of the door.

Thief 2 And then?

Thief 1 All the time a wicked rascal was up in the roof throwing needles at me and shouting, 'Cut him! Cut him!'

Thief 3 So what did you do then?

Thief 1 I ran, but a fellow with a thick whip beat me round the legs.

Thief 4 I'll never go back there myself, Leader.

Thief 5 You wouldn't catch me going in there either, Leader.

Thief 6 Nor 1, for all the gold in the world.

Narrator The six thieves all turned pale when they thought about what had happened. Then they all ran as fast as they could across the river, up the valley and away. They may still be running for all I know.

Next day — in the cottage

White Pet Good morning, my dear friends.

Bull Good morning, White Pet.

Dog Good morning, White Pet.

Cat Good morning, White Pet.

Chicken Good morning, White Pet.

Goose Good morning, White Pet.

White Pet I have had an idea. I think that we six friends should all live here in this cottage and make a better life for ourselves together.

Narrator And the other five agreed. For all I know the six friends are still living in that little stone cottage in Scotland.

Some questions to answer

1 What had made White Pet, Bull, Chicken and Goose run away from their homes? What were they afraid would happen to them?

2 Why had Cat and Dog run away from their homes? What were they afraid would happen to them?

3 What had each of the six friends set out to find?

4 Who was already in the cottage and what were they doing?

5 Who was the 'man' with green eyes who stabbed the leader of the thieves in the hand?

6 Who was the 'man' with huge teeth who blew out the candle?

7 Who was the bully in the thick woollen coat?

8 Who was the fat brute who was behind the door of the cottage and threw out the Leader of the Thieves?

9 Who was the wicked rascal who was throwing down needles from the roof?

10 Who was the fellow with the whip who beat the Thief round the legs as he ran away?

Some things to draw or paint

1 A silhouette is an outline picture, the figures in a silhouette are usually coloured in black. They look like shadows against a wall. Draw or paint a silhouette of Dog or Cat.

2 In the mountains of Scotland, as well as flocks of sheep and

herds of cows, there are deer wandering freely about. The stag, or male deer, has large horns called antlers. Draw or paint a picture of a stag on a Scottish mountainside.

3 The Union Jack is the flag of Britain. It is made up of the red crosses of St. George and St. Patrick and the white cross of St. Andrew. St. Andrew is the national saint of Scotland. The Scottish flag just has the cross of St. Andrew of it. Draw or paint the flag of Scotland.

A puzzle to solve

1 Bull used to sleep in this when he lived on the farm.
2 Dog used to shelter in this when he was cold and tired.
3 Cat liked to be in this room in the house.
4 Chicken always slept here before she left home.
5 Goose ran away and left this.

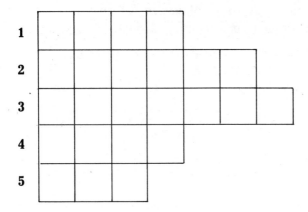

Discover : Scotland

You will need to look at a map of Scotland to be able to answer most of these questions.

1 There are two sections of Scotland: the Highlands and the Lowlands. Which part of Scotland do you think is called the Highlands? Is it (a) the south (b) the north?

2 What are the names of the two largest cities in Scotland? Which one is the capital of Scotland?

3 What are the names of the groups of islands (a) to the north east and (b) to the north west of Scotland?

4 Why do you think there are not many towns along the north western coastline of Scotland?

5 On the map you will see the following words used a great deal: 'Ben' and 'Glen'.
Does 'Ben mean (a) river (b) lake (c) mountain?
Does 'Glen' mean (a) moor (b) valley (c) forest?

6 There is a large area of water in Scotland called Loch Ness. What does 'Loch' mean? What might you find in Loch Ness?

The Scottish people

In Scotland there are groups of people who belong to 'clans'. Find out (a) what a clan is (b) some names of different clans (c) the name given to the head of a clan (d) how you would recognise that people belong to different clans.

3 *Odysseus and the Cyclops*

Greek stories

In Greece about 3000 years ago there were people who were very interested in art, drama, poetry, science and ideas. Many of the subjects that are taught in schools all over the world came from ideas that these people had developed.

The Ancient Greeks believed that their gods and goddesses behaved like ordinary people except that they had great strength and power and lived forever. The Greeks told stories about the way the gods and goddesses took an interest in the lives of the people who lived on earth. Their stories were about heroes and warriors who went on long and dangerous journeys or fought in terrible wars.

One of the greatest Greek writers was a poet named Homer. He wrote two books called, *The Iliad* and *The Odyssey*. *The Odyssey* tells the story of the hero, Odysseus, who was the favourite of some of the gods and disliked by others. His fortunes went well or badly depending on which of the gods was the most powerful at any one time.

Odysseus and the Cyclops

Odysseus, the Greek warrior, and his band of men are sailing home after years of fighting in the Trojan Wars. The voyage is long, difficult and dangerous. When they land on the island of the Cyclops people, they begin looking for food and water. It is while they are searching that they find something worse than they could ever have imagined.

Characters:

Odysseus	**Ilion,** *friend of Odysseus*
Greek Woman	**Delos,** *friend of Odysseus*
Greek Man	**Cyclops Man**
Diomede, *friend of Odysseus*	**Cyclops Woman**
Adamas, *friend of Odysseus*	**Cyclops Warrior**
Polyphemus, *the Cyclops Giant*	

Greek Woman A long time ago a great and brave man called Odysseus was travelling home to one of the Greek islands after years of fighting in a war.

Greek Man He travelled with the men who had fought at his side. They sailed through dangerous seas.

Greek Woman They met many monsters who were cruel and strong. One of these was the great giant of the Cyclops people.

Greek Man The giant's name was Polyphemus.

Greek Woman Odysseus and his men were exploring the Cyclops' island. They did not know about Polyphemus. This is what happened.

On the beach of a small island

Odysseus Come, men, let's find out what the island is like.

Adamas Some of the men should stay to guard the ship but I want to explore with you, Odysseus.

Ilion I want to go with you too, Odysseus.

Diomede So do I.

Delos And I.

Odysseus Then I shall take you four and eight more. The rest must stay here to protect the ship.

Greek Man They prepared for their exploration. They

35

took with them a goatskin filled with wine and they set out towards a very large cave.

Odysseus The cave is much bigger than it looked from the beach.

Adamas It seems empty. Let's go inside and see what we can find.

Odysseus We shouldn't wander too far away from each other in case there's danger.

Inside the large cave

Ilion There are baskets of cheeses in the corner, over there.

Diomede There are some young lambs and goats in a pen, at the back of the cave.

Delos And near the entrance there are some huge pails filled with milk.

Adamas Odysseus, we can have a feast. Let's eat then take the rest back to the others at the ship. Then we can set sail again.

Odysseus No, Adamas, we aren't thieves. We'll wait for the master to return, he may well give us what we need.

Greek Woman So they waited for the master to come back. They did not know that the master was the dreadful giant, Polyphemus, who had the strength of twenty men.

Odysseus My friends, do you feel the earth tremble and the sound of sheep bleating?

Adamas The owner of the cave must be returning.

Ilion He is no ordinary man. Just feel how the floor shakes like some great earthquake.

Diomede (*points*) Look! A huge creature has blocked the entrance to the cave.

Delos It's a giant as tall as a temple and as wide as a house.

Adamas And he has just one eye in the middle of his ugly forehead.

Ilion May the gods help us! A one-eyed giant with great strength!

Diomede We can't escape, he's rolled a stone right across the entrance.

Delos Maybe he's a gentle giant, look at the way he strokes the sheep and goats.

Odysseus Gentle or not, we mustn't disturb him. Just sit quietly and wait.

Greek Man So Odysseus and his friends watched as Polyphemus worked. Then the giant lit a fire and the flames threw light onto Odysseus and the others.

Polyphemus Ho! What do I see? What are you doing in my cave? What men are you? What is your name?

Odysseus We are men of Greece who are travelling home. We ask you to give us food and shelter.

Polyphemus Me? Give food and shelter? I give food and shelter to no one!

Greek Woman Then the giant, to show that he was no friend, seized two of the men and threw them to the ground. They died as they hit the stone floor.

Adamas No! I cannot watch, Odysseus. (*covers his eyes*)

Ilion Do something, he is going to eat them!

Diomede What can we do, Ilion, he is too strong.

Delos Odysseus, save us! He will surely kill and eat us all.

Greek Man Odysseus and his remaining ten men watched with horror as the giant sat down and rubbed his fat belly. Then he lay down to sleep.

Adamas Odysseus, let's kill him while he is sleeping.

Odysseus No, then we'd be as good as dead ourselves.

37

Ilion Why?

Odysseus It's only the giant who can move the great stone blocking the entrance to the cave. If he is dead then we die in here with him.

Diomede Then we are lost. If he lives he'll kill us, if he dies we're trapped.

Greek Woman The men spent a dreadful night weeping for their lost friends and listening to the giant's loud snores.

Greek Man In the morning, Polyphemus milked his goats and sheep. Then another awful thing happened.

Ilion No! No! He's going to kill more of us!

Adamas He's seized two more men.

Diomede He's eating them!

Odysseus Keep calm, do nothing, we must wait and take our chance when we are ready.

Delos He's pushing the great stone away from the entrance.

Diomede He's taking the animals out – quick now is our chance!

Odysseus No, Diomede, wait! You'll be crushed by the rock, see he's already rolled it back into place.

Adamas Now it's quite dark in here again. What shall we do, Odysseus?

Odysseus I have an idea. Help me to cut a spear from that tree trunk lying over there.

Ilion Well, you've led us for all these years, Odysseus, we must trust you.

Diomede Do you think you'll be able to save us?

Odysseus Work now and talk later. Sharpen this end of the wood until there is a good point.

Greek Woman They worked hard all day until the spear was ready. Then they hid it and waited.

Odysseus He's coming! Feel the earth shaking?

Delos I am so afraid, Odysseus, our battles were never as bad as this!

Diomede	There are only eight of us now left here with you, Odysseus, surely we aren't strong enough to kill this giant?
Odysseus	We must be brave. Trust me and trust our gods.
Greek Man	Then the stone was rolled back and the light shone into the cave. The goats and sheep trotted in.
Greek Woman	Then Polyphemus did his work. He sat down for a while then smiled and ...
Adamas	Help us, Odysseus! He has taken two more of the men!
Odysseus	Quiet and calm! We can do nothing for them. Remember the plan we have; we must wait before we act.
Polyphemus	Ho! Ho! You strangers have brought me good food! I like it! I'm happy to have you here! (*rubs his belly*)
Odysseus	We've got wine here too.
Polyphemus	What? Wine, did you say? I like wine, where is it?
Adamas	We have it here.
Polyphemus	Give it to me.
Odysseus	We have filled a pail with wine. Here it is. (*holds it up for Polyphemus*)
Ilion	Look how he snatches it! He's drunk it in one gulp!
Polyphemus	Good! That was good! I want more.
Greek Woman	So the giant drank more and more of their strong wine until he was quite drunk.
Odysseus	You remember, great giant, that you wanted to know our names, well, I'll tell you my name now.
Polyphemus	Did I want to know? Well, what is your name?
Odysseus	My name is Nobody. My friends' names are Nobody too.
Polyphemus	Nobody! A good name. Nobody, yes I like

	it. Then, Nobody, remember this, I shall eat each and every one of you weak, tasty little Nobodys.
Adamas	He's almost asleep, Odysseus. The wine is working.
Diomede	He's beginning to snore.
Ilion	Shall we fetch the spear now, Odysseus?
Odysseus	Yes! Then heat it up in the fire to make it stronger. (*they hold the spear in the hot ashes of the fire*)
Delos	The spear is ready now, Odysseus!
Odysseus	Every man must help. All together now, lift the spear and throw it at the giant's head. Aim for his eye! (*they throw the spear*)
Polyphemus	Oh! My eye! My eye! My wonderful eye! I cannot see. Help me! Help!
Greek Man	Polyphemus bellowed and shouted so much that the Cyclops people woke. They ran from their village to the cave.

Outside the cave

Cyclops Man	What is wrong, great giant?
Cyclops Woman	Is anyone trying to steal your sheep?
Cyclops Warrior	Who is trying to kill you?
Cyclops Man	Answer us, great giant.
Cyclops Woman	Who is hurting you?
Cyclops Warrior	Who is making you cry out like this?
Polyphemus	Nobody! It's Nobody. Help me, it's Nobody.
Cyclops Man	Oh well, if nobody is there, he must just be having a bad dream.
Cyclops Woman	If it's nobody at all then the giant is making fools of us.
Cyclops Warrior	If it's nobody at all then keep quiet, old giant, and let us sleep.
Greek Woman	So the Cyclops people went away not understanding what the giant was saying

	to them.
Greek Man	Next morning Polyphemus could see nothing at all. But he heard the sheep and goats bleating to be let out. Odysseus and his men waited for their chance.

Inside the cave

Odysseus	Now, listen to me. I shall tie each one of you to the belly of one of the fat sheep. Then I shall tie a sheep on either side of your sheep.
Adamas	We'll be hidden then beneath the middle sheep.
Ilion	Do you think the plan will work?
Diomede	If we are all silent and let the sheep walk out of the cave as usual, then it will work.
Delos	He cannot see a thing now and even if he feels the sheep, he won't be able to feel us.
Adamas	And what about you, Odysseus, how will you escape?
Odysseus	I shall take care of myself.
Greek Woman	So the plan was put into action. The men were tied beneath the sheep and the sheep bleated to be let out.
Greek Man	The giant rolled back the stone for them to leave the cave.
Polyphemus	Come, my sheep and goats, I cannot see you. I am in great pain but you must go out today and eat sweet grass.
Greek Woman	Odysseus watched as the sheep and goats trotted out. He held back the biggest and strongest ram by the horns.
Greek Man	Then he slid beneath the ram's belly and hid in the long wool.
Odysseus	Right then, my fine ram, carry me out of the cave.

Polyphemus	Let me feel you before you go, you are my best ram, I know that. I'd know that bleat of yours anywhere, even though I cannot see you. Now out you go, take care of the sheep and goats for me. (*pats the ram*)
Greek Woman	So the best ram trotted out to join the others. Odysseus held on tight, until they were well away from the cave.

Outside the cave

Odysseus	Men! We are safe, we are free!
Adamas	Untie us, Odysseus.
Ilion	Are we really free, Odysseus?
Diomede	Where is the giant now?
Delos	He could still catch up with us before we reach the boat.
Odysseus	Calm, be calm! We are all safe and free. Polyphemus is still in his cave and we will all reach the boat in safety.
Adamas	We owe you our lives, Odysseus.
Odysseus	We must give thanks to the gods! We will need their help again, I fear, before we reach home.
Greek Man	Odysseus was right, their adventures were not over. They had many more fierce monsters and dangers to meet.

Some questions to answer

1 What had Odysseus and his men been doing before they landed on the island of the Cyclops people?
2 What was the name of the giant who lived on the island?
3 How did Odysseus and his men know that someone was living in the cave?

4 Odysseus and his men could have killed the giant while he slept. Why did they decide not to do this?
5 How did they decide they would use the tree trunk, that was lying in the cave, to help them?
6 From where did the giant get the wine to drink?
7 What was the result of Odysseus' plan?
8 The Cyclops people ran to the cave but they did not help the giant. Why was the giant not given help?
9 How did Odysseus get his men out of the cave?
10 Which animal did Odysseus use to get himself out of the cave?

Some things to draw or paint

1 The giant, Polyphemus, had just one large eye in the middle of his forehead. Draw or paint a picture of what you think he might have looked like.
2 Polyphemus lived on an island. Draw an outline map of the island showing the following things: the bay where Odysseus' ship was anchored; the cave where Polyphemus lived; the grassland where the sheep and goats went to eat the grass; the town where the Cyclops people lived.
3 Before Odysseus reached home, he met more dangerous things. In Greek stories there are many monsters and dreadful beasts, some are half man and half animal. Others have hair made out of wriggling snakes. Draw or paint a picture of a monster that you would not like to meet.

A puzzle to solve (see over the page)

1 Polyphemus lived inside here.
2 Odysseus took this number of men with him to explore the island.
3 Odysseus told Polyphemus that this was his name and the name of his friends as well.
4 Polyphemus was given some of this to drink.
5 These animals helped to bring the men safely out of the cave.

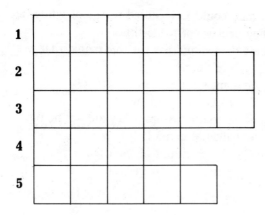

Discover : Greece

You will need to look at a map of Greece to be able to answer most of these questions.

1 What are the names of three countries that have a border with Greece?
2 Where is the capital of Greece and what is its name?
3 What do you think is the most important physical feature of Greece. Is it (a) rivers (b) islands (c) lakes?
4 Find out the names of three of the larger Greek islands.
5 Many years ago the Greeks believed that their gods lived on top of a large mountain. This mountain is the highest point of land in Greece. What is it called?
6 The Greek word 'poly' means 'many'. The word is used in English. Find out the meanings of these words which have 'poly' in them: polygon, polytechnic, polyglot, polygamy, polysyllable.

The Greek language

Greek writing does not use the same letters as most European languages. Try to find out the Greek signs and names for the letters: A, B, C, D. Try to write out your name using Greek letters.

4 *The Salty Sea*

Welsh stories

Many Welsh people are able to speak two languages: English and Welsh. Welsh is a very old and beautiful language. It is quite different from English and it belongs to the Celtic group of languages. It has close links with the languages spoken by the Irish and Scots and by people in some parts of Cornwall and Brittany.

For hundreds of years Welsh people wrote poetry and songs in their own language. The poems and songs told the stories that had been handed down from one generation to the next. Many of the stories were about great heroes and magical beasts.

When the English took control of Wales, the Welsh people were made to learn to speak English. Because they loved their old stories, the Welsh translated them into English so that they could still go on telling them. Because these stories have been translated, it is now possible for more people to enjoy them.

The Salty Sea

Three Welsh brothers have different ideas about how they should lead their lives. One of them receives a handmill which would usually be used to grind salt or pepper. There is something very special about this particular handmill that will change all their lives. It will also change the sea in a way that they could never have guessed.

Characters:

Narrator	**Old Man**
Gwyn	**Landlord**
Mair, *Gwyn's wife*	**Servant**
Bryn, *Gwyn's brother*	**Mr Thomas**
Glynis, *Bryn's wife*	**Sailor**
Lyn, *Gwyn's brother*	(*Someone to squeal and grunt like a piglet*)

Narrator Long, long ago when the world was still new, the sea was fresh water. At that time three brothers lived in Wales. Their names were Bryn, Lyn and Gwyn. This is their story.

A small cottage in the hills

Bryn When I grow up, I shall be a farmer. I shall grow good crops and have fine sheep and pigs.

Lyn When I grow up, I shall be a sailor. I shall have my own boat and sail the Welsh Sea and catch fish and lobsters.

Gwyn I don't know what I shall do when I grow up. I think I'll just be happy to walk up and down the lanes of Wales.

Narrator The years passed and the three brothers grew up. Bryn became a rich farmer. Lyn caught plenty of fish and bought a fine ship. Gwyn was happy doing nothing very much.

A large farmhouse

Bryn What a fine year we've had, good crops to harvest.

Glynis And we got a good price for the animals at the market.

Bryn We deserved to do well.

Glynis We've worked hard not like Gwyn, that lazy

47

brother of yours, and his awful wife.

Bryn Oh no! (*stares out of the window*)

Glynis What is it?

Bryn Gwyn and Mair are walking up the path right now!

Glynis They've come to get a free meal from us again. I can't stand this much longer.

Narrator Gwyn and Mair knocked at the door and came into the farmhouse with smiles on their faces.

Gwyn Hallo, brother Bryn, it's good to see you.

Mair How cosy it always is in here.

Gwyn Any chance of a meal, Glynis, we're ever so hungry?

Glynis You always are, as I recall!

Bryn Sit down then, the two of you, we were just going to have supper.

Mair That's nice!

Bryn Tell me, Gwyn, if I gave you that plump little piglet that you've been looking at ever since you came in, would you make me a promise?

Gwyn Yes, we'd do almost anything for such a plump little piglet, anything you asked.

Bryn Fine, then you can have the little piglet on one condition.

Mair What's that?

Bryn That neither of you set foot in this house for a year.

Gwyn Alright then, Bryn, we promise. We won't see you for a year.

Mair Shall we stay for supper though?

Bryn No! (*handing Gwyn the piglet*)

Glynis No! (*opening the door*)

Narrator So off went Gwyn, Mair and the plump little piglet. Bryn and Glynis danced together for joy! Gwyn and Mair walked along the lanes and up the hills.

Later — outside a small stone-built cottage

Gwyn There's an old man by the door, Mair, let's ask him if he knows where we can get a meal.

Mair He's got a long white beard and he's dressed like a shepherd.

Old Man Good evening, friends, what can I do for you and your plump little piglet?

Gwyn We're looking for somewhere to have a meal and maybe a room for the night.

Old Man The place you want lies over the next hill.

Mair Oh, so it's not far to go then?

Old Man No, not far. The landlord will welcome all of you but especially the plump piglet. Take my advice, will you, do not part with the piglet for anything he might offer you.

Mair Not for anything?

Old Man For nothing except his old handmill.

Gwyn But an old handmill is worth less than a plump piglet.

Old Man You do what I say and you won't be sorry. If you get the handmill, come back and see me and I'll tell you all about it.

Narrator So off went Gwyn and Mair with the plump little piglet. Soon they came to the place the Old Man had told them about.

A country inn

Servant There's a couple of strangers here at the door, Landlord, and they've got a plump little piglet with them.

Landlord Why so they have! What luck! I was just dreaming about roasted piglet.

Mr Thomas So was I, Landlord. A juicy pork chop would suit me just fine!

Servant Me too.

Landlord Let them in then, don't keep them outside in the cold.

Mair Good evening.

Gwyn We wondered if we could have a meal and a room here?

Landlord You're welcome.

Narrator So they all sat round the blazing log fire and warmed their hands.

Landlord That's a fine little plump piglet you've got there. I'll give you a red hen in its place.
(*piglet squeals and grunts*)

Mair Oh no, Landlord, what would we do with a red hen?

Gwyn We don't want a red hen. But we'll give you the plump little piglet if you give us the old handmill near the door.

Landlord The handmill! It's a broken old thing, no good to anyone at all.

Narrator The hours went by and nothing more was said.

Servant Oh my stomach is empty, Landlord.

Mr Thomas I can feel fat juicy pork chops in my mouth, Landlord!
(*piglet squeals and grunts*)

Landlord Hush! I can taste pork crackling too!

Mair Just one old handmill and you can have the plump little piglet.

Mr Thomas What's the matter with you, Landlord? Give it to them.

Servant We've never used the handmill.

Landlord Alright then. One handmill for you and one piglet for me.

Gwyn It's a deal!
(*piglet squeals and grunts*)

Narrator So everyone was happy – except the plump little piglet.

Gwyn Come on, Mair, back to the Old Man to find out the handmill's secrets.

Mair I hope it was worth it, Gwyn, I'm starving

myself.

Narrator   Off they ran up the hill and then down the
other side till they came to the cottage.

Back at the small stone-built cottage

Old Man   Ah! I see you took my advice and got the
handmill. You won't be sorry!

Gwyn   Tell us about the handmill, Old Man.

Old Man   Just you say, 'Little mill, pretty mill, be good
to me. Give me...' Then you tell the handmill
what you want and it will get it for you.

Mair   How exciting! I can't wait! I can't wait!

Gwyn   Let's try it then 'Little mill, pretty mill .....'

Old Man   Wait! Don't start until you know how to stop
the mill. When you want to stop the mill you
must say, 'Little mill, pretty mill, be good to
me, enough is enough'. Now off you go and try
it out.

Narrator   Mair and Gwyn laughed and ran and skipped
until they were tired.

Later — on a cliff overlooking the sea

Gwyn   Shall we try it?

Mair   Oh yes!

Gwyn   Little mill, pretty mill, be good to me. Give me
a fine house by the sea.
(*a house appears*)

Mair   Look! Look! There's a house. Now ask it for
some tables and chairs.
(*tables and chairs appear*)

Gwyn   Some carpets.
(*carpets appear*)

Mair   A horse, a cow, a pig and some hens. Oh look!
Look!
(*animals appear*)

Gwyn   Little mill, pretty mill, be good to me, enough

51

is enough!

Mair I can't believe our good fortune. What a fine house, what fine things!

Gwyn Tomorrow we must ride over in a fine new carriage and horses to see Bryn!

Mair No, we must wait a year. Remember our promise. And this time we must ask them to visit us here, not go to them. We can repay their kindness to us in the past.

Narrator One year later, Bryn and Glynis rode up the path that led to Gwyn and Mair's fine house. They could not believe their eyes!

Inside Gwyn's and Mair's fine house

Glynis I don't believe it?

Bryn I'll find out just how he did it. We'll know their secret.

Glynis It's not right that they should have done so well.

Bryn You keep that silly Mair talking and I'll get the secret out of that lazy brother of mine.

Glynis What a lovely meal, Mair! Could you show me round the house now?

Mair Good idea, then Gwyn and Bryn can chat together.

Bryn Let's have some more wine, Gwyn, then you can tell me how you did it.

Gwyn Did what?

Bryn Got all this money!

Gwyn It's all due to you really!

Bryn Due to me? How could that be?

Gwyn It was that plump little piglet that did it!

Narrator Then Gwyn told his brother everything, everything about the handmill. Except for one thing which he forget to tell him – the command words to stop the mill grinding. Then Gwyn fell fast asleep in front of the fire.

Bryn You stupid man! That handmill is going to belong to me. You're too stupid to know what to do with it. (*seizes the handmill*)

Later

Glynis Mair has gone to bed. Have you found out anything?

Bryn Shush! Not so loud or you'll wake him! Yes, I've found out what I need to know.

Glynis Good, then let's be off before they both wake up.

Bryn You get your things ready and I'll get into the carriage and wait for you.

Glynis This is exciting, I won't be long.

Narrator Bryn climbed into the carriage. While he waited, he thought he would try out the handmill which he put on his knee.

Bryn Right then! Little mill, pretty mill, be good to me. Give me a lovely woman to sit on my knee! Good job old Glynis isn't here! (*laughs*)

Narrator At once a beautiful woman appeared in the carriage, then another and another until the carriage was full of women.

Bryn Right mill, that's quite enough! Stop it! Stop it!

Glynis (*comes out to the carriage*) Whatever is going on! Get those women away from you, you beast!

Bryn You don't understand.

Glynis I do! Take that! And that! (*hits him*)

Bryn Oh! You've made me drop the mill. Where is it? Where is it? Glynis stop hitting me. We need the mill.

Narrator Women of every different size and shape were appearing because the mill had not been told the right words. They all chased after poor Bryn. Glynis was at the head of them.

Mair (*wakes*) What is all that yelling, Gwyn?

Gwyn It's Glynis beating Bryn over the head. But

more important than that, have you seen the handmill?

Mair No, isn't it behind the door?

Gwyn No. Bryn must have taken it. That's why there are women running all over the place.

Mair (*points*) There it is lying on the ground! Little mill, pretty mill, be good to me. Enough is enough.

Narrator The mill stopped. But Glynis went on chasing after Bryn. For all I know she is still chasing him!

Gwyn Let's not invite them here again, Mair.

Mair No, never again. Next time we ought to have your brother, Lyn, here.

Narrator One year later, Lyn sailed his ship to the shore near their house.

Lyn Well, brother Gwyn, you've done well for yourself.

Gwyn Yes, we have done well and we're very happy.

Lyn How did you do it?

Gwyn We've had good fortune.

Mair Bryn and Glynis were here and they tried to steal our little handmill.

Lyn Steal your handmill? What would they want with a broken down old handmill?

Gwyn It's the handmill that gave us all this.

Lyn How did it do that?

Mair It grinds out everything we need.

Lyn Does it indeed!

Narrator Then Gwyn told him the whole story, except he forgot to tell him the words to stop the mill grinding. That night Lyn crept out of bed.

Lyn That handmill is going to be mine. Why should that lazy brother have it? He doesn't know what work is. (*seizes the handmill*) Here it is! Now back to the ship.

On the ship

Sailor You're back! Do we sail now?
Lyn Yes, we sail.
Sailor Where are we going?
Lyn Out into the open sea.
Sailor Aye, aye, Captain.
Lyn Now then, let's see what this handmill can do. Little mill, pretty mill, be good to me. Give me some fresh salt to use with my catch of fish.

A few minutes later

Sailor Captain, a lot of salt has spread over the decks.
Lyn I know, it's coming from the mill. Clever, isn't it?
Sailor Captain, the salt is filling up the hold.
Lyn Alright, I'll stop it. Thank you, mill, that's all.
Sailor Captain, the ship is getting too heavy. Stop the salt coming out.
Lyn (*shouts*) Stop grinding! Stop it!
Sailor Captain, we're sinking! Jump for it and swim. (*jumps overboard*)
Lyn Oh no! My lovely boat! (*jumps overboard*)
Narrator The boat sank, but the handmill went on grinding out salt. When Gwyn and Mair woke up they looked for Lyn, then they looked for the handmill.

Back at Gwyn's and Mair's house

Mair It's gone again, Gwyn, so has Lyn.
Gwyn Well, perhaps it will do him some good. We've got all we need to live a comfortable life.
Mair Maybe that's true. But you've got a bad couple of brothers.
Gwyn Let's go for a swim.

Mair Alright, why not? I like to swim in that lovely fresh water. It tastes so good too.

Later — on the beach

Narrator They ran and skipped across the beach and dived into the water.
Gwyn Ugh! The water tastes horrible!
Mair Ugh! It is horrible and it's getting more salty every minute.
Narrator And for all I know the little handmill is still grinding out salt. So if you are ever by the Welsh Salt Sea, you know what you've got to say, don't you?

Some questions to answer

1 When Bryn was a boy, what did he decide to be when he grew up?
2 What did Lyn say that he wanted to be when he grew up?
3 What did Gwyn say that he wanted to do when he was older?
4 Why were Bryn and Glynis tired of having Gwyn and Mair at their house?
5 What was the deal that Bryn and Glynis made with Gwyn and Mair?
6 How did Gwyn and Mair know what to ask for in exchange for their plump little piglet?
7 What did Bryn ask for when he got hold of the handmill?
8 What happened when Bryn could not stop the handmill?
9 What did Lyn tell the handmill to give him?
10 What happened when Lyn could not stop the handmill from working?

Some things to draw or paint

1 Wales is sometimes called the 'Land of Song' because the people enjoy singing. The musical instrument that they often use to accompany the singing is a harp. Find out what a Welsh harp looks like then draw or paint a picture of one.

2 Salt, pepper and coffee are used in the kitchen. Nowadays most people buy their salt and pepper ready ground for them. However, some people still have handmills to grind out fresh salt, pepper and coffee. Find out what a handmill looks like. Draw or paint a picture of a handmill on a kitchen table.

3 Years ago, most goods were brought into Wales on ships like Lyn's. Now lorries also bring things into Wales. Many of these lorries cross the long Severn Bridge which connects England to Wales. Draw or paint a picture of a long bridge crossing a wide river.

A puzzle to solve

1 This was the name of Bryn's wife.
2 This was given to Gwyn and Mair to keep them away from Bryn's home.
3 Bryn asked for one of these to sit on his knee.
4 Lyn asked the handmill to give him some of this.
5 This man warned Lyn that the ship was sinking.

Discover : Wales

You will need to look at a map of Wales to be able to answer most of these questions.

1 Where are the largest number of towns and cities to be found in Wales? Is it in (a) the north (b) the south (c) the west?
2 Try to discover why most of the towns and cities are in that area.
3 There are a large number of rivers in Wales. Name *two* that flow into Cardigan Bay and *one* that flows into the Bristol Channel.
4 There are mountains in most parts of Wales. Where are the highest mountains to be found (a) the south (b) the north? Find the highest point and then find out its name.
5 There is an island off the North Wales coast. What is its name and what stretch of water separates it from Wales?
6 What beast does the national flag of Wales have on it?

Welsh history

In several parts of Wales there are large castles e.g. Harlech, Conwy, Caernarfon. Find out when and by whom they were built. What was the reason for them to be built? Why is the eldest son of the King or Queen of England called the Prince of Wales?

5 *Anansi and Old Witch Five*

West Indian stories

Hundreds of years ago there were people living in the West Indies called Caribs and Arawaks. They were hunters and fishermen. In the fifteenth century, Europeans landed on the islands and some of them decided to settle there. There was fighting between the Europeans and the Caribs and Arawaks and many of the native people were killed. Others caught the diseases that the Europeans brought with them and they also died. Today there are very few Arawaks or Caribs living in the West Indies. However, some of their folk-tales have lasted and are still told by the people who live there now.

The Europeans wanted to plant special crops on the islands. They needed workers to cut down the large forests and plant the crops. So they brought over thousands of people from Africa to do this work. These people brought with them their own stories and tales.

Anansi is the name of one of the characters in the new stories that are told in the West Indies. Anansi is a spider but he often behaves just like a man. He is nearly always very naughty and selfish. He is also very clever indeed.

Anansi and Old Witch Five

Anansi, the spider, lives in the West Indies on the same island as Old Witch Five. One day he overhears the old witch casting a spell. Then trouble begins for everyone when Anansi tries to use the spell himself.

Characters:

Anansi	Anansi's Child
Narrator	Mr Frog
Old Witch Five	Mrs Lizard
Grizzle, *the Witch's helper*	Tom Sharp
Mrs Dove	Mary Goodley
Anansi's Wife	

Narrator In the West Indies there is an island where the sands are silver, the sea is blue and warm, and the sun is hot. On that island lives Anansi, the spider. Also on that island lives Old Witch Five. This is their story.

Inside the witch's den

Grizzle Witch Five! Witch Five! There are two people waiting to see you. Witch Five!

Old Witch Five Hush your mouth! I heard you the first time, no need to yell!

Grizzle But, Witch Five, I said that...

Old Witch Five I know what you said.

Grizzle Shall I send them in? They are customers, Witch Five.

Old Witch Five There! You've said it again! Don't do it. (*waggles her finger at him*)

Grizzle Do what? Say what? I don't know what you're talking about, Witch Five.

Old Witch Five Agh! You've said it again! (*stamps her foot*)

Grizzle What?

Old Witch Five My name, you foolish child! I'm sick of the sound of that name! I hate it, I hate it! Don't use it again!

Narrator Grizzle creeps away from the Witch's brew room and goes to fetch the two customers.

Grizzle Hurry up, Tom. Hurry up, Mary. The Witch isn't in a very good mood.

61

Tom Sharp	Oh, I can see her, she's stirring her old black pot.
Mary Goodley	I don't like this place it smells horrible.
Grizzle	Well, go on, Tom, tell her what you've come for.
Tom Sharp	Witch, I've come for a powerful spell.
Old Witch Five	What for?
Tom Sharp	To make my sugar cane grow.
Old Witch Five	You don't need a spell, you just need to work harder.
Tom Sharp	Oh, Witch Five, please, help me.
Old Witch Five	Agh! He said it! He said it! (*stamps her foot*)
Tom Sharp	Witch Five . . .
Old Witch Five	Get out, go away before I turn you into something nasty and creepy. Get away, I say! No spells for you today. (*shoos him away*)
Tom Sharp	I'm going, Witch Five, and there's no money for you either.
Grizzle	Clear out, Tom Sharp, before the Witch does what she says. Now, you go to see her, Mary Goodley. Take my tip, don't use her name.
Old Witch Five	Well, what do you want?
Mary Goodley	Oh dear me! Oh dear me!
Old Witch Five	Stop saying that, girl. What do you want, eh?
Mary Goodley	Well, I, I, I . . .
Old Witch Five	What? What?
Mary Goodley	I want a spell to make me beautiful.
Old Witch Five	Beauty? Who wants beauty? It's brains you need, my girl.
Mary Goodley	Please, Witch Five, please . . .
Grizzle	Oh no! She's gone and said it!
Old Witch Five	Agh! Get out before I turn you into a toad. (*shoos her out*)
Mary Goodley	Oh dear me! Oh dear me!
Narrator	Mary ran from the room as Old Witch Five

	began throwing things round the room and howling dreadfully.
Grizzle	Don't throw things round the room, you're breaking the jars of spells.
Old Witch Five	They're mine, I made them, so I'll break them if I want to. (*throws a jar*)
Grizzle	Ow! That hit me!
Old Witch Five	I don't care! I don't care!
Grizzle	Well, you will care when all the money has gone. Tom and Mary left and we didn't get a penny.
Old Witch Five	I don't care! I don't care!
Grizzle	Whatever is wrong with you?
Old Witch Five	It's my name. I can't stand hearing it anymore. It's Witch Five do this. Witch Five do that. Five! Five! Five! I hate 'Five'.
Grizzle	Well, do something about it then. Change your name if it makes you feel so bad.
Old Witch Five	Why, Grizzle, how clever you are. That's just what I'll do.
Grizzle	Thank goodness, then we can get back to work.
Old Witch Five	I'll call myself, Witch Florizell. I like that, I like it very much.
Grizzle	Good, then that's settled.
Old Witch Five	No, Grizzle dear, not quite. I'm going to cast a spell on my old name so no one will ever use it again.
Grizzle	Alright then I'll fetch the spell book, Witch F. . Florizell!
Narrator	Now Anansi had been sitting there in the corner of the room as quiet as could be. No one saw him but he heard everything that had been said.
Anansi	What's that old Witch going to do with her spell, I wonder? It may be worth my while to hang around here and find out.
Old Witch Five	One dead rat!

Grizzle One dead rat! (*passes over the rat*)

Old Witch Five One cup of frog's blood!

Grizzle One cup of frog's blood (*passes over the cup*)

Old Witch Five One whisker from a walrus!

Grizzle One whisker from a walrus! (*passes over the whisker*)

Old Witch Five One squashed spider!

Anansi (*shivers*) Horrible!

Grizzle One squashed spider! (*passes over the spider*)

Anansi Horrible! (*shivers again*)

Old Witch Five Now let's stir them together in the pot.

Grizzle Round and round the pot they go!
Stir it back and to and fro!

Old Witch Five From now no more will stay alive!
Anyone who says the word 'Five'!

Grizzle Clever Old Witch Fi.. Florizell!

Anansi Ah Ha! So from now anyone who says you-know-what will no longer be alive. Could be very useful!

Narrator Anansi crawled quickly down the wall and ran home as fast as his eight legs could carry him to his starving wife and child.

Later in Anansi's home

Anansi's Wife Anansi, my husband, we are so hungry. When are you going to bring us food?

Anansi Hush, my little wife, don't worry. I'll be getting all the food you can eat very soon.

Anansi's Child Daddy, I can't wait. I'm so hungry!

Anansi's Wife Don't tease us, Anansi.

Anansi's Child Please bring home something good to eat, Daddy.

Anansi I'm off now, my little wife and dear child, I'll bring back the food.

Narrator So Anansi walks along the fields thinking up a plan. Then he jumps up and down and laughs.

On a dusty road

Anansi I've got it! I've got it! I'll collect corn and put it into four plus one little heaps. Oh, you clever boy, Anansi!

Narrator Anansi sat down in the road next to six, take away one, heaps of corn.

Anansi Looks like dinner is coming down the road.

Mrs Lizard Hallo, Anansi, what are you doing?

Anansi Mrs Lizard, I've worked so hard all day.

Mrs Lizard You poor old thing.

Anansi I'm taking all this corn to market, but it is so heavy.

Mrs Lizard Perhaps I can help you.

Anansi What a good idea. Let's divide the heaps into half, then we can take half each.

Mrs Lizard Good idea.

Anansi Trouble is, Mrs Lizard, I've worked so hard that I can't count anymore. Could you count the heaps for me?

Mrs Lizard Easy, Anansi, there's one, two, three, four, five. (*falls down dead*)

Narrator You know what happened! So that was Anansi's dinner taken care of.

Anansi Well, that was a good meal! I'll hide this corn under a bush until I need to use it again. (*rubs his tummy*)

That evening — in Anansi's home

Anansi's Wife Husband, where is the food?

Anansi's Child Daddy, dear, where is the food?

Anansi Sad to say, my little wife and darling child, there is no food today.

Anansi's Wife Perhaps I should work, Anansi, and you stay to look after our darling child.

Anansi's Child Perhaps I could work too.

Anansi No, my little wife and darling child,

	tomorrow is another day and I shall surely find food.
Narrator	Anansi went to bed and slept well. He'd eaten a great deal, hadn't he? So he felt quite tired! Next day!
Anansi	I am off to find food, my little wife and darling child.
Anansi's Wife	Come home soon, Anansi, and bring us food for me to cook.
Anansi's Child	Please, Daddy, please.
Narrator	Anansi skipped happily along the road to where he'd hidden the corn. He put it in seven, take away two, little heaps and sat down to wait.

Lunchtime — on the dusty road

Anansi	What a lovely day. I wonder who will come along the road this morning.
Mr Frog	Hallo there, Anansi. What are you doing there?
Anansi	It's alright for some, Mr Frog. But I've been working hard since early this morning.
Mr Frog	I can see that, Anansi. What a lot of corn you've collected.
Anansi	It is a lot, isn't it? Trouble is, Mr Frog, I have a problem.
Mr Frog	What's that, Anansi?
Anansi	I can't count.
Mr Frog	Can't count! Why that *is* a problem! Shall I help you?
Anansi	That would be just fine.
Mr Frog	Right then here goes. One, two, three, four, five! (*falls down dead*)
Anansi	Ah ha! Here is lunch!
Narrator	After his lunch, Anansi pulled his hat down over his eyes, lay in the sun and had a good sleep. Later that evening!

Back at Anansi's home

Anansi's Child	Here comes Daddy! He's here, Mummy, he's here!
Anansi's Wife	Husband, you look so hot and tired.
Anansi	I feel hot and tired, my little wife.
Anansi's Child	Any food, Daddy?
Anansi's Wife	You can see there's no food, my darling child. Don't bother your Daddy. He will try again tomorrow.
Narrator	And the next day! Anansi waved goodbye to his wife and child.

Later — on the same dusty road

Anansi	This is becoming almost too easy. I'll just put my corn in eight, take away three, little heaps.
Mrs Dove	Hallo, Anansi, you are working hard. What are you doing down there? I can't quite see from up here in this tree.
Anansi	I am working hard, Mrs Dove, but then I have a wife and child to feed.
Mrs Dove	Can I help you?
Anansi	That would be nice.
Narrator	So Mrs Dove flew down and landed on one of the heaps of corn.
Mrs Dove	What can I do to help, Anansi?
Anansi	My poor brain has gone tired, Mrs Dove. Could you count the heaps for me?
Mrs Dove	Coo! Coo! Easy, Anansi. There's one, two, three, four and the one I am sitting on.
Anansi	So how many is that, Mrs Dove?
Mrs Dove	I just told you, Anansi. One, two, three, four and this one here.
Anansi	But how many is that in all, Mrs Dove?
Mrs Dove	Coo! That's easy. Four and this one here.
Anansi	So! How many is that?

Mrs Dove	Coo! It's the one I'm sitting on plus four others.
Anansi	(*crossly*) You stupid bird. You bird brain! Say it! Say it!
Mrs Dove	Say what, you rude spider?
Anansi	(*shouts*) One, two, three, four, fi....Oh!
Narrator	Now Old Witch Fi .. er .. Florizell had been watching all that Anansi was up to. She was angry that her spell had been used to get his food. So that morning she had put a stop to her spell. But instead she turned Anansi into a tiny, weeny, little spider right before Mrs Dove's eyes.
Mrs Dove	Why, Anansi, how tiny weeny you've grown! (*peers at him*)
Anansi	Blow it! Blow it! (*stamps his eight tiny feet*)
Mrs Dove	What's that, Anansi, I can't hear you? Your little voice is so small! Perhaps that will teach you not to call me bird brain.
Narrator	Then Mrs Dove pecked up the corn for her lunch. Anansi ran home as fast as his tiny, weeny, eight legs would carry him.

Back at Anansi's home

Anansi	Wife!
Anansi's Child	Mummy, I heard a squeak. What was it?
Anansi's Wife	I heard nothing.
Anansi	Wife!
Anansi's Child	There it is again, Mummy.
Anansi	It's me, your darling father!
Narrator	Anansi's child and wife peered at the tiny, weeny, little spider sitting on the floor. Then Anansi's wife picked him up and peered even closer.
Anansi's Wife	Why, Husband, I see it is you. You're going to take quite some time to grow up into a big spider again. Luckily you won't

be needing much food.

Anansi's Child What shall we do for food, Mummy?

Anansi's Wife Why, my darling child, you and I will get food for ourselves. Your tiny, weeny father will have to sit here at home and wait for us.

Anansi's Child Why is that, Mummy?

Anansi's Wife Such a tiny, weeny spider is not safe in the big wide world.

Narrator And that night Anansi's child and wife had a lovely meal of sweet corn and sugar and baked fish. Anansi just watched and kept very quiet.

Some questions to answer

1 At the beginning of the story, Old Witch Five is very cross and upset. Why was she so upset?

2 What did Tom Sharp want to get from the Witch?

3 Grizzle was worried when Tom and Mary left so quickly. What was worrying him?

4 The old Witch decided that she would have to do something about her problem. What did she decide to do?

5 Anansi overheard the spell being made. How did he decide to use it for himself?

6 Who was the first animal that Anansi tricked into counting his heaps of corn?

7 Who was the second animal that he tricked into counting his heaps of corn?

8 Why did Anansi get so cross with Mrs Dove?

9 What did Mrs Dove do with the corn when Anansi became tiny weeny?

10 What do you think of the way Anansi treated his wife and child?

Some things to draw or paint

1 Anansi lived on an island in the West Indies. There are many islands that make up the West Indies. Some are large, others are quite small. Draw an outline map of an island and then mark in on it: mountains or hills; a river or a lake; beaches and some small towns.

2 Because of the climate in the West Indies certain crops and fruits grow very well. There are bananas, oranges, grapefruit, rice and sugar cane. Draw or paint a picture either showing some of these crops and fruit growing in the West Indies or showing the fruits on a plate.

3 There are many different types of spider. Some have large hairy bodies and short legs, others have small smooth bodies and long thin legs. Some spiders are plain brown or black, others have coloured patterns on their bodies. Draw or paint some of the different types of spider that you have seen.

A puzzle to solve

1 This animal was the second one to be tricked by Anansi.
2 Tom and Mary both wanted one of these from the old Witch.
3 This person helped the old Witch to do her work.
4 This was the naughty spider's name.
5 This bird was not able to count the way that Anansi wanted.

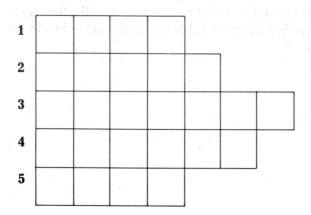

Discover : West Indies

You will need to look at a map of the West Indies to be able to answer most of these questions.

1 The West Indies are made up of several islands stretching over a large area of sea. Make a list of three West Indian Islands.
2 Which is the largest of the West Indian islands?
3 What is the name of the sea that lies between the West Indies and South and Central America?
4 The West Indies are quite near the Equator, they are also surrounded by large areas of sea. What type of weather do you think these islands have?
5 In greengrocers' shops there are several fruits and vegetables that come from the West Indies. Find out the names of some of these fruits and vegetables.
6 The West Indian people are fond of music. Some of their music has become very popular in other parts of the world as well. Name a type of music that comes from the West Indies.

The history of the West Indies

Find out why so many places in the West Indies have Spanish, French or English names. All the people who now live in these islands did not come from this part of the world originally. Their grandparents and great grandparents were from another continent. Find out where they came from originally, then try to find out why they left their old homes and went to live in the West Indies.

If you have enjoyed reading the stories in this book and would like to read more stories from other countries, here are some books which will interest you:

Indian Tales and Legends by J.E.B. Gray (Oxford University Press, 1979)
Scottish Folk Tales and Legends by Barbara Ker Wilson (Oxford University Press, 1975)
Heroes of Greece and Troy by Roger Lancelyn Green (Bodley Head, 1975)
Welsh Legends and Folk-Tales by Gwyn Jones (Oxford University Press, 1975)
Fairy Tales from Here and There by Amabel Williams-Ellis (Blackie and Sons Ltd, 1977)